Anne Fine

Illustrated by Philippe Dupasquier

How To Write rEallY BAdLY

EGMONT

First published in Great Britain 1996
by Methuen Children's Books
Reissued by Egmont Books Ltd 2002
239 Kensington High Street
London W8 6SA

Text copyright © 1996 Anne Fine
Inside illustrations copyright © 1996 Philipppe Dupasquier
Cover illustration copyright © 2002 Lee Gibbons

The moral rights of the author and illustrators
have been asserted

ISBN 1 4052 0061 8

10 9 8 7 6 5 4 3

A CIP catalogue record for this title is
available from the British Library

Printed and bound by Cox & Wyman Ltd
Reading, Berkshire

You can visit Anne Fine's website,
www.annefine.co.uk, and download gorgeous
free bookplates from www.myhomelibrary.org

CoNTenTS

1 Bad News Bear   *1*

2 All goody-goody and
old-fashioned   *11*

3 Ugly stuff!   *17*

4 Trash or treasure?   *29*

5 Quieter around here   *40*

6 'Why are you torturing him
like this?'   *51*

7 The Golden Rules   *60*

8 A little, secretive, one-person
crime wave   *74*

9 Mad Model Movers PLC   *83*

10 By popular request . . .   *90*

1
BAd NEws BeAR

I'm not a total lame-brain. Nor am I
intergalactically stupid. And I don't go wimp-
eyed and soggy-nosed when bad things
happen to me. But I confess, as I looked round
the dismal swamp that was to be my new
classroom, I did feel a little bit cheesy. Oh,
yes. I was one definite Bad News Bear.

'Lovely news, everyone!'

Miss Tate clapped her hands and turned to
the lines of dim-bulbs staring at me over their
grubby little desks.

'We have somebody new this term,' she said.
'Isn't that nice?' She beamed. 'And here he is.
He's just flown in from America and his name
is Howard Chester.'

'Chester Howard,' I corrected her.

But she wasn't listening. She was busy
craning round the room, searching for a spare
desk. And I couldn't be bothered to say it

1

again. I reckoned she was probably bright enough to pick it up in time. So I just carried my stuff over to the empty desk she was pointing towards, in the back row.

'And that's Joe Gardener beside you,' Miss Tate cooed after me.

'Hi, Gardener Joe,' I muttered, as I sat down.

It was a joke. But he was clearly even more of a bean-brain than Miss Tate.

How to Write Really Badly

'Not Gardener Joe,' he whispered. 'Joe Gardener.'

I didn't have the energy to explain.

'Oh. Right,' I said. And my spirits sank straight in my boots, setting a personal (and possibly a world) record for getting to hate a new school. I've moved more times than you've watched *Sesame Street*. I've managed bookish schools, and sporty schools, and schools where the teachers keep hunkering

down to your level to look you in the eye and ask you how you *really feel*. I even managed four months in a school where no one else spoke English. But I never took against a place so fast as I took against Walbottle Manor (Mixed).

Some Manor! I reckon the building was designed by someone who was taking a rest from doing morgues and abattoirs. The walls were shiny brown and shiny green. (The shiny made it worse.) The windows hadn't been washed since 1643. And all the paintings pinned up round the room looked like eight sorts of pig dribble.

But, hey. Nowhere's *perfect*.

I gave Gardener Joe a nudge.

'So what's she like?'

'Who?'

I nodded towards the front.

'Her, of course. Crock at the top.'

He stared at me.

'Miss Tate? She's very nice.'

My turn to stare. Was my new neighbour

touched with the feather of madness, or what? Here was this epic windbag, droning on and on about whose turn it was to be the blackboard monitor, or some other such great thrill, and Gardener Joe was sticking up for her. I knew right away that this was the sort of school where everyone lines up quietly to do something really exciting, like opening the door for a teacher. And if you gave them something wild to play with, like a wobbly chair, they'd probably be happy all through break.

I looked at my watch.

'Six hours,' I muttered bleakly. 'Six whole hours!'

Joe Gardener turned my way.

'Six hours till what?'

'Till I can complain to my mother,' I explained.

'Complain?'

'About this place.'

His face crumpled up in bewilderment.

'But why complain?'

And he was right, of course. Why bother to complain? It never gets me anywhere. 'Marry the woman, marry the job,' my father always says.

'But I didn't marry her. You did,' I point out to him. 'So why should *I* suffer?'

'It could be worse,' he warns. 'Your mother could get fired. Then we might be stuck here for ever.'

That usually snaps me out of it pretty fast.

'You'll like it here,' this Joe was telling me. 'We do a lot of art.'

I stared at the pig dribble pictures.

'Oh. Very nice.'

'And we have fun at break.'

'Watching the puddles dry?'

Joe's puzzled look came back to take another quick bow. And then he finished up:

'And we have singing on Fridays.'

'No kidding? Not sure I can wait that long.'

But this Joe Gardener was turning out to be a bit of a sarcasm-free zone.

'I feel that way sometimes myself,' he said.

'But wait and see. It'll come round so fast.'

His eyes shone as if he were talking about his birthday, or Christmas.

'Singing on Fridays,' I said. 'Right. I'll remember that when things get grim.' And I looked up to see how we were doing with today's great excitement – choosing the blackboard monitor.

'So that's agreed, then, is it?' Miss Tate was saying. 'Flora this week, and Ben the week after.'

I suppose, when something of world-shattering importance like this is decided, it's always best to check things one last time.

'Everyone happy with that?'

I'd have put money on the fact that no dill-brain in the world could give a flying crumpet who was blackboard monitor, this week or next. But – whoa there! I was wrong. Quite wrong.

This hand beside me shoots up in the air.

'Miss Tate?'

'Yes, dear?'

'I think it would be nice if Howard –'

'*Chester*,' I couldn't help correcting.

But he wasn't listening. He was busy fixing my life.

'If Howard was made blackboard monitor. Because he's new. And I don't think he's very sure he's going to like it here. Because he's already worked out that it's six whole hours –'

See my eyes pop? But what was staggering me most was that this bozo meant well! He was trying to be *kind*!

'– till he gets home.'

I flicked on all exterminator rays, but nothing could stop him. He was being *nice*.

'So I think it would be a really good idea if we made him blackboard monitor.'

Joe sat back, satisfied.

Miss Tate spread her hands like someone glowing in a holy painting.

'Flora? Ben? Would you mind?'

Surprise, surprise! Ben didn't burst into tears, and Flora didn't gnash her teeth at not

being blackboard monitor for one more week.

So, that's it. Ten minutes in, and I'm Head Wiperoony. What Great Luck!

'Well!' Miss Tate said brightly, giving me a meaningful smile. 'My blackboard looks as if it could do with a thorough good wiping, just to start the day.'

I sighed. I stood up. What else could I do? I took the little furry wooden block from Flora's outstretched hand, and smiled back sweetly when she smiled at me. I wiped the board, then set the little furry thing carefully on its ledge.

'Very good,' Miss Tate said. 'Excellent. A

lovely job.'

You'd have thought that I'd balanced the budget, or something.

Modestly, I wiped the chalk dust from my fingertips.

'And now let's give Howard a nice big round of applause as he goes back to his desk.'

I didn't put up any further fight. Chester. Howard. What's in a name? I was a broken reed, ready to slip my head in a noose, or walk the plank, or do anything I was asked. Don't get the wrong end of the stick. I am no wimp. I've smacked heads in my time. Young Chester Howard here has stuck up for himself in schools where the pudding plates go flying, and schools where, if you don't watch yourself, someone's infected teeth are in your leg, and schools where the staff need cattle prods.

But Walbottle Manor (Mixed)! Their sheer bloodcurdling *niceness* had defeated me, and I ran up the white flag.

Howard it was.

2
ALL GOODY-GOODY AND OLD-FASHIONED

You wouldn't *believe* the playground. Half of these goofballs were wandering round offering their last crisp to anyone who looked in the slightest bit peaky, and the rest were all skipping.

No kidding. They were skipping. Two rosy-cheeked milkmaids in pigtails were swinging this great long rope, and everyone else was jumping up and down, all thrilled to bits, waiting their turn.

Then, each time someone rushed in under the rope, everyone burst into song.

I stood on the steps and listened. First I heard:

Miss Tate bent down to pick a rose.
A rose so sweet and tender.
Alas! Alack! She bent too far,
And bang! *went her suspender.*

And then I heard:

Mandy Frost was a very good girl;
She went to church on Sunday
To pray to God to give her strength
To kiss the boys on Monday.

I turned to Joe.
'Is this some kind of special day?'
He trotted out his puzzled look.
'What do you mean?'
I didn't quite know how to put it.

'What I mean is, are you all pretending to be sweet little orphans, or something? Is this some sort of History Day?'

I wasn't ringing his doorbell, you could tell.

'History Day?'

'You know. Like when all the girls dress up in pinafores, and everyone sits with their arms folded neatly on their desks, and the teacher pretends that it's a hundred years ago.'

A light came on in his attic at last.

'Oh! Like when we did our Victorian School Day?'

I shrugged.

'Whatever. Something all goody-goody and old-fashioned, anyhow.'

He stared round the playground. In one corner, two of the bigger boys were putting their arms round a sobbing toddler who'd lost his pet marble, or something. By the porch, boys and girls were practising a hornpipe. (I am *serious*.) Next to the gates, a gaggle of merrymakers were doing a complicated clapping game. And all the rest were ambling around, smiling and waving to one another, or loyally waiting for friends outside the lavatories.

'What I mean is,' I said, 'where *are* we? On the planet *Zog*?'

Joe's eyes lit up.

'Oh, yes! That would be fun. Let's both be visitors to the planet Zog, and you – '

I gave him my hardest killer stare. Who did this blintz-brain think I was? Some bedwetter, keen to play his Betsy-wetsy games?

'Listen,' I said. 'I think maybe it's time that

How to Write Really Badly

I explained something to you.'

But he'd clapped his hand to his mouth.

'Oh, Howard,' he told me. 'It'll have to wait till after break. Because I've just remembered I promised Miss Tate I'd help her cut the covers for our new How-to books.'

And just at that moment, the lady herself appeared on the steps.

'Jo-ey!' she warbled. 'Jo-ey Gardener!'

'Coming, Miss Tate!' he trilled.

And he was off.

I slid my back down against the nearest wall and sank my head in my arms. Oh, just my luck. I've made my way in schools where the uniform is so itchy it brings you out in hives, and schools where you have to stand and pray five times a day, and schools where they make you do your work over and over again, until it's right.

But never had I fetched up somewhere like this. Already I could hear the scuffling of anxious little feet. Nervously I looked up, and found myself encircled by worried faces.

Anne Fine

'Howard?'

'Are you all right?'

'It's difficult for anyone on their first day.'

'You'll soon get used to us, honestly.'

'Do you want to come and skip?'

I opened my mouth. I was about to speak. The first words were just rising to my lips when the bell rang.

Just as well . . .

3
UGLY stuff!

An hour later, Miss Tate explained the whole soul-rotting business again, for any beef-brains who weren't listening the first ten times.

'So here are your lovely covers, which Joe has very kindly helped me cut to size.'

Our Joe took his tenth bow.

'And paper is on my desk. Lined here, and unlined here.'

She pointed twice, just in case anyone in the room was so deeply brain damaged they were going to get in a tizzy, searching for something in a space one metre by two.

'And all of you get to choose what you write about. But it does have to be a little How-to book. So it could be – ?'

She pointed to Beth.

'How to keep rabbits,' Beth said promptly, and beamed.

(This wasn't news. We had been through

Beth's plans at least a zillion times since we'd trooped in.)

'Or how to – ?'

She pointed at some of the crawlers in the front row, and they jumped to it again.

'How to make a kite.'

'How to start your own candle factory.'

'How to grow mustard and cress.'

'Train your dog.'

'Plan a night's camping in winter.'

'Decorate hard-boiled eggs.'

I've fallen in some time warp, I know I have. And now Miss Tate is working her way back through the class to me and Joe.

She points at him first.

'Joe? How to – ?'

He looks all worried.

'I haven't thought of anything yet, Miss Tate.'

Now she looks all worried as well.

'Howard?'

I should have answered her, I know I should. But I was too busy stabbing my desk with

my pen point and muttering 'Chester!' darkly under my breath.

'Oh, deary me!' she said. 'It looks to me as if that's *two* of you still without any ideas. Maybe I should run through it one more time . . .'

I started to growl. And it was in the balance for a moment, till she glanced at the clock. But clearly one small corner of her brain had not yet been steeped to mulch by staffroom tea, because she suddenly had a fresh idea.

'Why don't I come and talk to you two on your own?'

I turned the growling up a notch. But old Two-Legs-No-Brain at the next desk looked absolutely thrilled.

'She's coming over to help us!'

He said it the same way you or I might have said, 'Free videos for life!' I stuck my finger to the side of my head and swivelled it, to let him know I thought he was some forlorn turkey. But then a shadow fell across my desk, and there stood Miss Tate in a cloud of moths, beaming at both of us.

'So what's it going to be, boys?'

How to Write Really Badly

'Mine's a secret,' I told her.

That got her off my back, and on to Joe's.

She made a steeple of her fingertips.

'Now, Joe. Isn't there anything that you'd enjoy using the library to learn about?'

Joe picked at his fingernails and shook his head.

'Well, how about something you've always thought there ought to be a little How-to book about?'

Joe was busy recycling his earlier performance as Baffled Man.

'Surely there's something you've always wished you were good at?'

'Counting to three without having to take off your mittens?' I suggested.

'Howard!'

Miss Tate was shocked, you could tell. She raised an eyebrow you could hatch bald eagles in. But just at that moment Joe the Thimble-brain thought of something at last.

'I wish I could write more neatly.'

Miss Tate patted his head as if he were some

starved, three-legged puppy she'd found in a
lost dog pen.

'I think we all wish you could do that, Joe.'

He looked up hopefully.

'So shall I choose it?'

'What?'

' "How to Write Neatly." I could have a try.'

'Well, yes, Joe. You could have a try . . .'

She didn't sound overly confident. But, fired
with enthusiasm, he opened his work book.
And suddenly I saw why Miss Tate had had
her doubts. This Joe beside me was The Writer
From Hell. I tell you, the day the teachers at
Walbottle Manor give gold stars for
penmanship away on the roof, this Joseph
Gardener will have the stairs to the basement
all to himself.

'Wow-ee!' I drew my breath in. 'That is *ugly
stuff*!'

'Howard!' Miss Tate warned.

But no one can stop you staring. The pages
in Joe's work book were clotted black and
nasty. A troupe of drug-crazed centipedes in

leaking ink boots had clearly held a barn dance over most of them. The rest looked tidy in comparison. (Not tidy enough to *read*. Just tidy in comparison.)

'I think we're talking high hopes here,' I couldn't help observing to Miss Tate. 'Reach for the stars, and all that. "Writing More Neatly" is well down our Joey's page of contents, if you ask me. I think he ought to stick with "Learning to Write".'

For all this was Happy Class, her tone turned pretty frost-topped.

'I'll thank you to pipe down, Howard Chester,' she said. 'Joe here does have the odd little problem with his schoolwork, but he's struggling along manfully.'

'Manfully?' I snorted. 'Scruffily and messily, more like!'

Joe flicked back to the pages in the front.

'I'm definitely improving,' he insisted. 'See how much better and neater my work is since I started special lessons twice a week with Mrs Hooper?'

I took a look. I looked in the front of the book, and I looked in the back.

'That Mrs Hooper is one brave, brave lady,' I observed.

Miss Tate said warningly:

'I'm losing patience with you, Howard.'

So I stowed it till she left. Then all I did was watch as poor cack-handed Joe picked up his pen, gripped it so hard his hand looked like some paralysed tarantula, and wrote, pitifully slowly:

How to Write Really Badly

'That won't do,' I told him. 'There's five mistakes in that. Not to mention the truly dismal standard of penmanship.'

Joe tried to stick up for himself.

'But you can read it, can't you?'

'Of a fashion.'

'It's the best I can do.'

'Then you're writing the wrong book,' I told him patiently. 'Always, in project work, it's best to trade on your strengths, not on your weaknesses.'

Joe sighed.

'Not sure I have any.'

If you don't mind, I'm breaking off to make a short public service announcement here. I *know* when someone says to you, 'I'm not sure I have any strengths,' you're supposed to pat their paw kindly and say to them: 'Of *course* you do! *Everyone* has strengths. It's just that some people's are more hidden than others.

And some people's don't show up in
school.'
I *know* you're supposed to say that.
OK? It's just that that isn't what
I said.

What I said was:
'Oh, I don't know. You're really good at
writing really badly.'
You want to know my big mistake? I'd said
the magic words: 'You're really good at –'
That was my big mistake. Here was this sad
case at my side, whose teachers probably
hadn't drawn a smiley face at the bottom of
his work since he was *three*, and I was saying
he's really good at something.
'Do you think so?'
He beamed so wide, I thought his face
might split. For one grisly moment, I feared
he would even lean over and hug me.
Then it was Worry Hour again.
'But will you help?'
So tell me, all you bigheads out there

reading this: what would you have said? Here I am, stuck in Happy Valley School, where everyone is peachy-sweet, and this poor dimple-head thinks that I'm being *nice*, like everyone else.

I'd like to see you wriggle out of it any better than I did.

'Sure,' I said. 'I'll help.'

I picked up my pen. I wrote the title in big, clear capitals, so he could copy it on to one of the bits of card he'd spent break cutting to make covers. And copying isn't hard, so he made quite a decent job of it. I won't say it was neat. And there were way too many fingerprints. And he'll take time to crack this business of the backwards 'e'.

Anne Fine

But I was proud of it. And so was he.

After a bit, Miss Tate trills over our way:

'So how's it going, Joe?'

He sticks his tongue back in his mouth to answer her.

'It's going well. Howard is helping me.'

Now didn't Miss Tate look pleased at that!

'And, Howard, how about your own work?'

'It's still a secret, Miss Tate.'

'Well, just so long as you're getting on with it.'

I looked at my nice white cover on which, so far, I'd written diddley-squat.

'Getting along nicely, Ma'am.'

She nods away, all happy as a clam. My mother's always saying it, and it is true. Some of these teachers are so away with the fairies, they should be put right out to grass.

4
TraSH or tREasurE?

I would have found it easier to work in a street riot. You wouldn't believe the noise Joe Gardener made, trying to write. His pen clattered to the floor ten times a minute. He said 'Sorry!' half a dozen times whenever he stabbed me with his elbow. And every few seconds he lifted his desk lid and rooted through the garbage inside.

It was like sitting next to a giant gerbil.

'What is the matter?' I asked finally.

He turned his worried face in my direction.

'What do you mean?'

I tried the question round another way.

'Why aren't you working?'

'I *am* working. You can *see* I'm working.'

'No,' I said. 'I can't see you working. All I can see is you knocking things off the desk, and flapping your paper, and lifting your desk lid every ten seconds to stir up the

29

mess inside.'

'Well, I am working.'

'You've got nothing done.'

And it was true. So far he'd managed:

I felt a little brutal. He looked crushed.

'What is that, anyway?' I asked.

'What?'

'What you've written.'

'Can't you read it?'

I gave it my best shot.

'Ik you ore?'

He sighed so heavily, I knew I'd got it totally wrong. I tried again.

'Ik –'

'*If.*'

My turn to stare.

'*If?*'

He pointed.

'That's an *f*.'

How to Write Really Badly

'In your dreams!'

'Be fair,' he argued. 'That is definitely an *f*.'

'And I'm a wombat.'

His face dropped.

'Well, that's why I was looking in my desk. Somewhere I've got a special sheet of paper with a lot of words written out for me.'

I peered into the dark abyss that was Joe Gardener's desk.

'How could you ever find one special sheet of paper in that tip?'

Flushing, he tried to defend himself.

'I'm looking for my dictionary as well.'

I dipped a finger in and gingerly stirred a few mucky papers about.

'No sign of any books in here.'

'Maybe it's sunk to the bottom.'

'Why don't you clear it out, for heaven's sake? Then you'd be able to find things.'

He said unhappily:

'I do *try*. It's just –'

His voice trailed off. It didn't matter, though. I didn't really need telling. I'd seen him take a million years to (try to) write three words. If someone like Joe tried clearing his desk, he'd have a beard down to his feet before the job was done.

I pushed my blank How-to book cover aside.

'All right,' I sighed. 'Let's get on with it.'

'But we're supposed to be –'

I didn't stop to listen. I just punted up the front to fetch the waste-paper bin. Miss Tate's beady eye fell on me the moment I stretched a hand under her desk.

'Howard?'

'Just borrowing the bin,' I explained.

'But, Howard. That bin's for everyone.'

I think what I hate most about being in school is being treated like a halfwit.

'Yes. I do understand,' I said. 'But, right at this moment, Joe and I need it most because he can't get down to work until we've cleared out his desk and found his dictionary.'

A strange light flickered in her eyes.

'Cleared out Joe Gardener's desk?'

I think I got the look right. I think my

expression clearly said, 'Yes, lady. You get the pay cheque. I do all the work.'

No more trouble from her, then. I carried my trophy back, and planted it on the floor beside Joe's desk. Then I pointed to my chair.

'You sit here.'

He shifted over. (Putty in my hands.)

'Right,' I said, lifting out the first disgusting sheet of chicken-scratchings. 'Trash or treasure?'

'Trash,' he admitted.

I lifted another. 'Trash or treasure?'

'Trash.'

This is my mother's trick. She uses it on me three times a year, before my grandmother's visits.

'What about these?'

'Trash. Trash. Trash. Trash.'

It took a while. I had to keep putting my foot in the bin to stamp the rubbish down, and make more room. But gradually we worked our way down all the tides of rubbish in his desk. And once or twice we had a

nice surprise.

'Treasure! I lost that pound *weeks* ago!'

Or:

'My dental appointment card! Mum's been nagging me for that!'

And suddenly, a triumph!

'Hey! That's my special sheet of paper!'

'Take a break.'

I strolled across to Flora.

'Borrow your sticky tape?'

Miss Tate had spotted me.

'Howard,' she trilled. 'We don't go wandering in this class without putting up our hands first, to ask permission.'

What is it with teachers and this stupid 'we' business? Miss Tate had been rolling round the room all morning, and never once put up her hand.

'Gosh, sorry!' I warbled, and scuttled back with Flora's tape in hand. I used a lot. (No point in messing about.) I stuck that special sheet of paper on the desk so well it won't go walkabout again. And I took a look at it.

How to Write Really Badly

once knew called guess
ready caught night garden
school hospital break doing

That sort of thing. And maybe I was in a mood because I hadn't had time to get started on my own work.

'Oh, right,' I muttered. 'All the really *hard* words.'

Joe lifted his face.

'That's right,' he said gratefully. 'All the words where it's easy to make mistakes.'

So I admit it. Though I didn't smirk, I was still feeling pretty superior as we ploughed through the silt at the bottom of his desk.

'Trash or treasure?'

'Trash.'

'Into the bin. And this?'

He reached for it in relief.

'My dictionary!'

'Just try to keep it near the top in future.' (Miss Tate could take lessons from me.) 'Is that the lot?'

He took the last thing I was holding up.

'Trash.'

He dropped it in the bin, and was about to put his foot on it when I reached down and snatched it.

'What is this?'

'It's just a photograph.'

'I know it's a photograph, Bean-brain,' I told him sharply. 'But what *is* it?'

He shrugged.

'It's just a model that I made last year.'

'Just a model?' I inspected it. Then I inspected him.

'Excuse me,' I said. 'But may I ask you a very personal question? If you can make a three-metre model of the Eiffel Tower from macaroni, why can't you keep your desk tidy?'

'I don't know.'

'Well, I'm sure I don't.'

I was still staring at him when the bell rang. I hadn't got any work done. But I'd achieved something. I'd shifted a major health hazard in the next desk. I'd got to know the worst writer in the world. And I'd worked out he wasn't daft.

Not bad for my first morning, you'll admit.

5
Quieter around here

I soon found out why he'd been sitting alone before I showed up to take the last desk. Come silent-reading time, my hand spent more time flapping in the air than turning pages.

'Miss Tate. Joe's sound-it-outs are getting on my nerves.'

'He's driving me *mad*, Miss Tate. No one could read against his mutterings.'

'I've read exactly four pages. Exactly *four*. Each time he starts up, I have to go back to the top of the page.'

Miss Tate laid down her marking pen.

'Joe. Please try and do your sound-it-outs more quietly.'

He went even redder than he was before.

'I *am*. You'd practically need an ear-trumpet to hear me, Miss Tate.'

'Howard can hear you well enough.'

'I most certainly can,' I burst out. 'C-a-t,

cat. D-o-g, dog.'

'That isn't fair,' said Joe. 'I'm reading about camels.'

When I got home that night, I asked my dad:

'What's *wrong* with him, anyway? How can he have enough of a headful of brains to walk and talk, and not be able to write "would" and "could" without making eighty mistakes?'

'Wiring,' my dad said darkly. 'Faulty wiring. A bit like that flat we rented in Rio.'

I nearly died in a fire in that flat. So next day, back to school, I made an effort to be more sympathetic.

'Look,' I said. 'Either you get your act together a bit, or I will murder you. Which is it to be?'

'I *try*,' he said. 'I really *try*. It's just that some things don't *stick*.'

'It's not as if you're *stupid*,' I complained. 'If you were *stupid*, we'd know where we stand.'

'I'm sorry. I'm sorry.'

I got the feeling he'd been saying it since

he was born.

'Oh, never mind,' I snapped. 'I'll work something out.'

And some of the things I worked out went quite well. That afternoon I tackled *should* (along with *would* and *could*).

'Start it with one of your ghastly little sound-it-outs, and then remember "Oh, you little darling" for the end.'

'Oh, you little darling?'

'O-U-L-D.'

How to Write Really Badly

'Brilliant!'

Then his face fell.

'But how do I remember which words it works on, Howard?'

'Try putting them in a rhyme.'

And suddenly it was drama night at the next desk. Joe Gardener was pulling an imaginary cloak around his shoulders, twisting his face into an evil leer, and saying to me cruelly:

Oh, you little darling!
You know you would *if you* could,
And you should!

I pushed him off smartly. He fell on the floor.

'I hope you two aren't distracting one another,' called Miss Tate.

We kept our heads down for a bit. I tried to get on with my work, but over and over my eyes were drawn to Joe's 'How to Write Really Badly' book. I tell you, this boy works like a duck with a shovel. It is so horrible, you have to watch. And, after about a billion false starts, he'd only got this far.

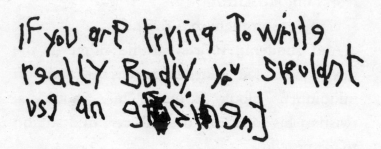

I pointed to the last big filthy smudge.

'What's this supposed to mean?'

'*Efficient*,' he said bravely. But he was worried, you could tell.

'Backwards "e"s,' I warned.

He fixed the 'e's.

'Now is it right?'

'Oh, no,' I told him. 'We're still miles from home.'

Sadly, he crossed it out, and wrote *good* above it.

'Why did you do that?'

'I always end up having to use the easy

words I can get right.'

'You can't do that. People will think you're a halfwit.'

'A lot of them think that anyway.'

'Well, that won't do, will it?'

I sat and thought for a while. And then:

'I've got it! ICI is an efficient company.'

'So?'

'So you can remember that.'

'Why?'

'Because,' I said triumphantly, writing it down in the big baby letters I had already learned to use for him, 'It sorts out the difficult middle bit.'

effi.c.i.ent

He stared at it for a while. Then:

'Got it!'

Maybe he had. Maybe he hadn't. (He'd be the last to know.) In grim fascination, I watched his slow, scruffy progress down the page, till the bell rang for lunch.

'Goody!' he said, stuffing things in his bag. 'Time to go home!'

'But we haven't had the afternoon yet.'

'Oh.' His face did fall. But I can't say he looked all that surprised. And, later, when it really was time to go home, he looked surprised all over again.

'He has no sense of time at all,' I told my dad. 'If you ask him the days of the week, he'll reel them off all right. But even if someone told him it was Tuesday yesterday, he still won't realise that it's Wednesday today.'

My father tossed chopped onion in the pan.

'How is he on the months?'

'He *says* he knows them. But he misses out November.'

'You get to Christmas sooner, I suppose. And what about the alphabet?'

'I don't know.'

'Ask him tomorrow.'

So I did. He had to sing it. But he sang it

perfectly. By G, I'd started conducting. And when he finished with a flourish on X, Y, Z, I said to him:

'If you know your alphabet as well as that, how come you have to spend the best part of a week riffling through your dictionary to find the letter you're after?'

'Singing's different.'

I reported back that night.

'He says that singing's different.'

And while my dad chopped parsley for the salad, I did my imitation of Joe Gardener scouring the dictionary for the letter W.

My dad looked up from the chopping board.

'Show you a trick?'

He took the dictionary from me.

'What do you bet that I can't turn to the M's in one go?'

'Nothing,' I said. (I'm not stupid.)

He opened the dictionary and showed me a page full of M-words.

'Very good.'

'And what do you bet me I can't find

the D's?'

'Nothing.'

He opened the book again, in the middle of the D's.

'Excellent.'

'Bet me I can't find the S's in one go?'

'I'm hanging on to my money.'

Just as well. He opened to the S's in one go.

He went back to his salad. I opened the dictionary, looking for E, and landed on F. Then I tried B and landed on A.

'So how did you do that?' I asked him finally.

'Old trick,' he said.

'But it's a new dictionary.'

'It works with all dictionaries,' he said. 'Open it right in the middle, and you're in the M's.'

I tried it. He was right.

'Now try exactly halfway to the end again.'

'Three-quarters through?'

'That right. You'll land on S.'

I did. Then I tried the first quarter, and

I landed on D.

'Works every time,' he told me.

'I'm impressed.'

Not half as impressed as Joe was, the next day.

'Do you realise that now you'll only have to riffle through a quarter of the dictionary each time you want to find a word?' I told him.

'So I will.'

He tried it, humming his little alphabet song under his breath.

'It works!'

'Of course it works.'

'You are so clever, Howard!'

'Thank my dad.'

Miss Tate interrupted our little festival of praise.

'Shouldn't you two be getting on with your work?'

Joey was radiant.

'Oh, really! We are!'

He might be, I suppose. I haven't actually got any work done since I came. My How-to book is still a total blank. But now he won't be riffling and humming quite so much, I suppose there's hope. At least it's getting quieter around here.

6
'Why aRE you TOrtuRing hiM Like tHIs?'

Within a week or two, I'd got his sloppy bag packing down to an art.

'So where are we going now?'

He'd look at everyone rushing through the door, brandishing their gym stuff.

'To games?'

(Sherlock the Second, this boy.)

'So what do you need?'

He wasn't allowed to say it until he had it safely out of his locker into the bag.

'Sneakers. Shorts. T-shirt. Socks.'

Then off we'd go to games. Not that there was much point. He wasn't very good at them. (I'm being nice, here. Joe was *terrible* at games. He was so bad that even Miss Tate's pack of Goody Two-Shoes had to grit their teeth not to groan aloud if he ended up on their team.)

And he was terrible at maths, as well. Whatever page of problems Miss Tate gave out to him, he'd sit there, fidgeting and sighing till my nerves were in tatters.

'So what's the matter *now*?'

'I don't get it.'

'*What* don't you get?'

(I don't know why I bothered. I might as well have asked someone who was stone deaf, '*What* can't you hear?')

'I just don't get it.'

Why should I work myself into a frazzle for free? Miss Tate gets paid for it.

'Miss Tate. Miss Tate! Joe's stuck again!'

You have to hand it to the lady. She did her best. Day after day, she'd haul the coloured rods and blocks over to his desk, and set them out, and go through the problems again.

'So, Joe. Let's take it step by step. This block here is worth –?'

'A hundred?'

She'd shake her head.

'A thousand?'

How to Write Really Badly

'No. Think, Joe. We went through this only yesterday.'

'Ten, then.'

Third guess lucky. Not that there was that much left to choose. But still Miss Tate managed to crank the enthusiasm up into overdrive.

'That's right, Joe! So if we don't have enough of the red blocks to . . . drone . . . drone . . . drone . . . drone . . .'

Joe tried. He'd nod. And carry on answering her step-by-tiny-step questions, one by one.

But there was no point in it. None of it *took*. The moment she walked away, he couldn't remember the right questions to ask himself, to get to the answer. He couldn't *understand*. And all the blocks and rods cluttering his desk were baffling him as much as the numbers that confused him in the first place.

'I reckon only the people who can do it in the book can do it with the rods and blocks,' he grumbled to me once.

'Spotted it right away, Joe!'

'So what's the point?'

I shrugged. 'Search me.'

Sometimes, just for a rest, she'd give him something he knew how to do. And *still* he'd get it wrong. I'd lean across to sort him out, and find he'd copied out the question wrong. This writing backwards business had crept into his numbers.

'You're supposed to be multiplying by thirteen, not thirty-one.'

'Am I?'

He'd spend ten minutes finding his

place on the worksheet.

'So I am!'

Not that he'd even get the answer after that. His next mistake was usually to copy the right number into the wrong place.

$$Example: \quad 43$$
$$+ \; \underline{154}$$
$$= 584$$

He'd go through it four times over, to be sure. Then:

'Have I made any mistakes at all in the adding?'

I'd check for him.

'No. No mistakes in the adding.'

'So it's *right*?'

'I'm afraid not.'

And I'd call Miss Tate over yet again, with all her rods and blocks, to try and explain.

One day, I asked her:

'Why are you torturing him like this?'

Miss Tate looked hurt and horrified.

'Torturing him? Howard, what on earth do you mean? I was just asking Joe if he *understands*.'

'But Joe doesn't *know* if he understands.'

'Maybe he'll get it suddenly. Some people do.'

She turned her back on me.

'So, Joe,' she said patiently. 'Let's try this one again. We start in this column, don't we? So what's seven times eight?'

We wait *forever*. And then, at last (because Joe can lip-read Beth) the answer comes.

'Fifty-six?'

How to Write Really Badly

Miss Tate was thrilled.

'Excellent, Joe!'

One mini-micro-second later, she's asking him:

'And what's eight times seven?'

And he's back to picking miserably at his fingertips.

'Come on, Joe. You just did it.'

'Did I?'

'Yes.'

'When?'

'Just now. You told me: "Seven times eight is fifty-six".'

'But I thought you wanted eight times seven now.'

'Joe, they're the *same*!'

He fakes it well enough. Slaps on his bright 'I-think-I've-got-it-now' face. And she pretends she's fooled (because that's her job). But I don't have to act the idiot.

'*See*? You're just torturing him. If he hasn't even grasped that seven eights is the same as eight sevens, how can you start him on *fractions*? It's not *fair*.'

'They're very *easy* fractions.'

'Thumbscrews are gentle compared with the iron maiden, I expect.'

'Howard!'

She's getting cross with me, I can tell. But I am cross with her. How can she carry on week after week, acting as if, deep down inside (if she could only reach it), Joe's brain is just like mine or hers? Why can't she see his clockwork doesn't tick like ours?

'He's getting a lot more right these days, aren't you, Joe?'

'That's just because Howard's helping me.'

'I'm sure it isn't.'

'Yes, it is,' I said.

'Howard!'

'It's true,' I insist. 'Joe gets along all right. But only by bluffing and guessing and mind-reading you, and lip-reading Beth, and getting answers from me.'

'I'm sure that's not true.'

'Ask him – if you feel lucky!'

How to Write Really Badly

She doesn't dare. She simply turns on her heel. And I know what I said hit home because, when she gets to her desk, she wheels round on me, and says, her face scarlet:

'I think perhaps I ought to move you, Howard.'

Joe's wail is pitiful.

'Oh no, Miss Tate! Don't separate us, please! I *like* sitting next to Howard! He's a great help to me!'

She doesn't push it. But later, when the bell rings, she takes my arm and draws me aside.

'I think maybe you'd do a whole lot better, Howard Chester, if you took less interest in other people's work, and more in your own.'

She had a point. For when I opened my How-to book to prove her wrong, it was still a blank.

7
THE GOLDEN RULES

'Today,' I told him, 'I am getting on with my own work.'

'Just start me off first,' he pleaded.

'No,' I said. 'I have to get on myself. Once I start with you, there's never any stopping.'

So, sadly, he set off in his brutish handwriting across the page.

People who write relly Badly

It's no good. I can't concentrate. I lay down my pen and slide the new photographs he's brought in to show me out of their envelope.

'I've said this before,' I told him. 'And I shall probably say it again. I don't understand how someone who can stuff eighteen jumbo-sized models into one tiny bedroom without breaking any of them can't copy one word

without losing his place half a billion times.'

I glanced at his work again.

'Or six words in a row without falling off the edge of the paper.'

Look how he'd finished this time.

People who write relly Badly hav

I touched his hand.

'Are these the fingers that built that three-metre Eiffel Tower out of spaghetti?'

'Macaroni.'

'Whatever.' I tapped his head. 'Is this the brain that worked out how to make his sister's Hallowe'en mask flash orange and green? Is this the same boy who stuffed all the speaker wires back in the right holes when Ben Bergonzi put his great hoof through them?'

'That's different,' he said sadly. 'I don't have to *learn* wires and glue and stuff.'

I shook my head.

'You're in the wrong place,' I told him. 'You shouldn't be here. It's sapping your confidence. You ought to be trailing behind someone who builds bridges, or invents light displays for famous bands on tour, or bugs other people's telephones.'

'I'd like that.'

'Never mind,' I said. 'Only –' I did a rapid calculation in my head. 'Only about one thousand, six hundred and forty-six days to go.'

He looked up, interested.

'Till when?'

'Till you can switch to doing what you're good at.'

Wistfully, he stared at the photos spread across the desk.

'One thousand, six hundred and forty-six days . . .'

I glanced at my watch.

'And this one's slipping away pretty sharpish,' I warned. 'So pick up your pen and get your own personal little Knucklehead Show back on the road.'

'I'm stuck.'

'Just have a go. No one's expecting you to win any prizes.'

'I won one once,' he said proudly.

'Really?'

I wasn't really listening. For suddenly, right then and there, I'd worked out exactly what to do with my own empty How-to book, down to the very last page.

But he was determined to tell me.

'Yes. I won a prize. Two years ago at the Summer Fair.'

He looked so proud that, even though I was desperate to get on with my idea, I couldn't help asking him:

'Which prize?'

'The prize for the boy who could keep his head in a hole longest while people threw wet sponges at him.'

Okay, then. I admit it. I'm not a *stone*. I have a heart. And I have heart-strings, too. And my little underachieving deskmate had just twanged them so hard they almost bust.

'Right-ho,' I said, picking up my pen. 'I'll help you.'

And pushing my own How-to book aside, I started off on his.

To write really badly (in Joe's chicken-scratching style) you'll need some paper – any grubby old scrap will do – and a pen that makes terrible blotches. Look for a lumpy place to work. (Rocks and laps are good, but runaway buses are better.)

Sit exactly right. Slouch to one side, and stick out your legs on both sides. Make sure you're in poor light, or can't see what you're doing over a pile of books.

Grip the pen so hard your knuckles go all white, and make sure you've twisted your hand round till you're almost writing upside down.

'I don't do that, do I?'
'Yes. Yes, you do.'

It's very important not to write any letter of the alphabet the same way twice. A really bad writer can make the same letter look completely different twice in the same word.

Example:

I handed him the pen.

'Go on, then. Do the example.'

'Me? I'm rotten at examples. You know that. I *always* get them wrong.'

'You're the only one who can get this one right.'

'Really?' His eyes lit up. 'What shall I write?'

'Write "pancake",' I told him. 'That has two letters the same in it. If you spell it right.'

He spelled it right because I told him how.

Example:

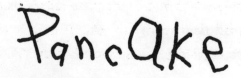

How to Write Really Badly

'Beautiful!' I said. 'Perfect! See what I mean? Always trade on your strengths. You'd never think those two "a"s were the same letter.'

'So can I do *all* the examples?'

'No one else but you.'

The next day, we did capitals.

Guess which of us wrote the examples on the top?

Right.

You can use capital letters to start people's names, and new sentences. But if you're trying to write really badly, you won't bother. (And try

*making some of your capitals smaller than little
letters. That'll fool people.)*
Example:

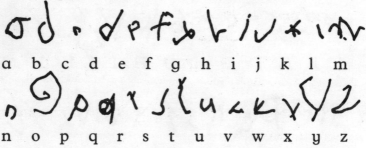

The day after that, we did small letters.

Guess which of us wrote the bottom ones?
Right again!

*To save time and effort, the end of one letter can
be used as the start of the next.*
Example:

How to Write Really Badly

Don't worry, you'll soon learn which letters don't matter at all, and can be left out completely.

The next day, we did special exercises.

Don't ever try to write two letters together the very same height.

Example:

sea
wrong ✗

ʃₒa
right ✓

And always make sure your tall letters slope in funny directions.

Example:

bdfhkL
wrong ✗

bdfhkL
right ✓

Try not to use lined paper because, if you're trying to write really badly, the last thing you want is everything neatly on one level.

Example:

paint
wrong ✗

paint
right ✓

And we did numbers, too.

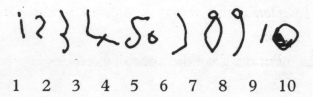

1 2 3 4 5 6 7 8 9 10

How about making your 5 look like a letter S? Or your 6 like an 0? Remember that really important numbers should be smudged*. And, for a nice change, why not write half the number as a word, and the rest as a number?*
Example:

(31)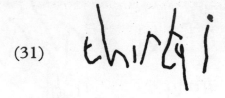

As you can see, this could easily be taken for 'thirty!'

I thought it was important to cover dotting 'i's and 't's.

The Golden Rules for dotting are:
1. Don't give a dot to anything that should have one.
2. Put it a few letters away (in either direction).
Joe provided the example.

So I thought of something else.

Always make sure that you have more dots than you need. The extra dots should be scattered just anywhere over the page of writing.

Then we went home.

After the weekend, we started on punctuation.

Too much punctuation is fussy and unattractive. Forget about question marks and exclamation marks, and be very mean indeed with commas.

*But you can sprinkle full stops anywhere in the
sentence (except at the end).*

Example:

Howard and. I are Nocking Hard

And then, just to finish it all off neatly, we did
spacing and layout.

*Always go right to the very edge of your
paper, even if you fall off. Any bright reader
will be able to guess what your last word
was going to be.*

Example:

After You Have a bath you are quit

*If you are sitting right, your work should slope
right up or down the page. Don't worry about
paragraphs. Esteemed chicken-scratchers never
worry about paragraphs.*

How to Write Really Badly

I handed the pen to Joe.

'Now write "Good Luck" to finish.'

Out popped the old tongue, and he wrote:

GOOD LUCK!

Then he studied the last bit more carefully.

'What's "esteemed"?'

'Respected. Honoured. Famous for something.'

'So,' Joe said, much taken with all this 'example' stuff he'd been so good at over the last few days, 'we could say, "*Example:* Joe Gardener is esteemed for writing really badly".'

(No way round this one.)

'We most definitely could.'

8
A little, secretive, one-person crime wave

Now Joe was finished with his own work, he started taking an interest in mine.

'Why are you sitting like that, all twisted round? Are you trying to write really badly?'

'No. I'm just hiding my work from you.'

'Why?'

'Because it's secret.'

He was hurt.

'I'll get to see it anyway, on Open Day.'

'But not till then.'

He shrugged. Then Mr Hurt turned into Mr Worrywart.

'It must be hard for you, writing bent round like that.'

'*You* manage perfectly well.'

'But I'm used to it.' His eyes lit up. 'I know! I'll make you a screen!'

He did, too. The very next day, he brought in a brilliant screen he'd made out of cornflake packets. It folded neatly when it wasn't up, and fitted in his desk. But whenever Miss Tate said, 'Time to get on with your How-to books,' he'd take it out and set it up between the two of us, lowering the flattened lavatory roll stabilising flaps, and swinging the empty cassette case stability buttresses round into place.

And it did the job perfectly. He couldn't see.

'Wonderful!' I said gratefully. 'That is so much easier.'

Miss Tate wasn't quite so keen on it, you could tell.

'Must you two have all this junk cluttering up your desks?'

'It's my security screen,' I told her. 'It helps me work.'

She sighed.

'I suppose I should just be thankful you've started at last.'

Started? Why, I was working like a *fiend*! I spent every hour I could checking my calculations, ruling perfect lines, and making sure my number work was flawless. Joe sat beside me, fiddling with scraps of cardboard and string and glue under the desk whenever Miss Tate wasn't looking in his direction, and worrying about me all the rest of the time.

'Do you think you'll be finished by Open Day?'

'I most certainly hope so.'

I wasn't sure, though, so I took it home and worked on it while Dad was making supper.

'What on earth is that?'

How to Write Really Badly

'This is my project,' I told him. 'It's a How-to book.'

'Oh, yes? How to *what*?'

'Survive in school.' I saw him staring. 'It's a present for Joe.'

Dad wiped the pizza dough off his fingers and flicked through the pages I'd done.

'This isn't proper work. All this is, is a heap of numbered squares.'

'It isn't just any old heap of numbered squares,' I said. 'By the time Open Day comes round, in that book there will be exactly one beautifully measured numbered square for every single day that poor Joe Gardener still has to spend in school.'

Dad turned to the last page, roughed out in soft pencil.

'One thousand, six hundred and forty-six?'

'We're really down to one thousand, six hundred and thirty-eight now,' I admitted. 'But still I thought it would be nice for Joe to cross a good few off right at the start.'

'That's all it's for? For Joe to cross them off?'

'Or fill them in with coloured pens.'

Dad was appalled.

'But what's the *point*?'

'It'll make him feel better. All prisoners do it. It helps them get to the end of their sentence without going out of their minds.'

'But Joe's not in prison. He's in Walbottle Manor (Mixed)!'

'He might as well be in prison. In fact, if he was in a prison, he'd have a better time. He'd enjoy fixing all the sewing machines they use to make mail bags, and inventing weird things for picking locks.'

Dad started thumping his pizza dough really hard.

'School's not a chain gang,' he protested. 'It is a worthwhile journey of the mind to a valuable destination.'

'Tell that to Joe!' I scoffed. 'To *him*, school is just somewhere he has to go because they make him, and when he gets there they just nag at him all day for doing everything wrong.'

Dad stabbed my How-to book with doughy fingers.

'I reckon he won't be the only one being nagged, the day Miss Tate sees this.'

I didn't argue with him. I was too sure that he was right. But I still kept on ruling out my perfect squares each time Miss Tate told us to get on with our projects. And sometimes even when she told us to stop.

'Pens down! It's time to plan the class

displays for Open Day!'

Joe gave me a nudge.

'You have to put your pen down now.'

'Nonsense,' I told him, carrying on ruling squares. 'Old Frost Top will never notice.'

But Old Frost Top did.

'Howard! You're last to put down your pen, so I'm afraid you'll have to run a little errand for me.'

Oh, joy! I'm out of here for five whole minutes! But, as I pass, everyone looks sorry for me, as if they think she's punishing me too hard. One thing you can be sure of, none of these wimpettes spent wet afternoons sticking pins in their dollies. Off I go.

I whistle up the corridor, around the bend, past the assembly hall, and into the secretary's office. No one is there. The list I'd come to fetch is lying on the table, though. *Miss Tate's Class: List of Open Day Prizes.* And then a heap of dreary, crudbucket honours.

How to Write Really Badly

Best Spelling
Best Essay
Best Reading
Best How-to Book
Best Number Work

No prizes for Joe in there. And then an idea struck. I snatched the scissors from the secretary's desk, and snipped off the bottom line – Whoops! Sorry, Beth! No prize this year! – and at the top, very carefully, I printed out:

Best Home-made Model

Then I went strolling back. Miss Tate was busy fighting a tragic avalanche of window display, and barely glanced at it.

'Just stick it up where everyone can see it.'

I prised a pin out of the pig dribble painting I hated most, and watched with satisfaction as it peeled off the wall and fell in the bin.

'There!' I said, using the pin. 'I now declare this class's List of Prizes officially on display.'

A second avalanche fell on Miss Tate. And what with her sticky tape rolling away under the desks, and all the fuss about what sort of glue she ought to use to stick the photo of Ben's mother's stuffed owl, Patricia, on to the nature display, nobody even noticed my own little, secretive, one-person crime wave.

9
MAd MoDel MOVers PLC

My mum put up a fight.

'In case you hadn't noticed, the firm I work for is called Hightechnicon Systems, not Huge Wobbly Models Removals Inc.'

'Joe's models aren't wobbly,' I told her. 'He's an expert.'

'Chester, it costs a fortune just to keep that van idle on the tarmac. Think how much it would cost to send it on your little errand.'

'It won't take long.'

'Loading and unloading.'

'I'll arrange all that.'

Moodily, she poked at her pasta. I was winning.

'Do this one thing for me,' I said. 'And I won't moan about any school I'm in – ever again.'

Dad's eyes lit up.

'Close the deal right this minute!' he ordered

Mum. 'Close the deal instantly, or it's divorce.'

Mum closed the deal. She made a couple of phone calls, and that was that. The van showed up outside Mrs Gardener's house early the next day.

'We've come for all Joe's models,' I told the cleaning lady. 'For the Open Day display.'

Eye lighting-up time is getting earlier and earlier around this neighbourhood.

'What? *All* of them?'

'All of them,' I said firmly.

'Even the wall-sized cooked tagliatelle spider's web?'

'Yes,' I said. 'And the disposable plastic coffee cup spaceman. And the fully spinnable tin bottle top Wheel of Fortune. And the personally collected driftwood crocodile.'

The cleaning lady trembled.

'So I'd be able to get in and vacuum under the bed? And wipe down the windowsill? And wash the walls?'

'The room will be all yours. As empty as a

summer desert drain till four o'clock. Just lead the way.'

She stopped tremulously halfway up the stairs.

'Will you be taking the dried bread lampshade?'

'Yes, we'll be taking that too.'

She clutched her light-bulb duster tightly in her emotion.

'Just along here!'

I wouldn't want to pass much time in Little Joey's bedroom. I wouldn't mind picking my way under the toilet roll holder flying rocket. Or through the papier-mâché Valley of the Kings. But I'd just hate sleeping directly underneath that filled plastic water bottle mastodon. Or waking up to put my feet by accident on to that jelly-filled freezer bag octopus.

'Is that the lot?' the driver asked, when I'd filled up the van.

Joe's mother's cleaning lady wiped what I could only take to be a tear of joy out of her eye.

'You promise me they won't be back till four o'clock?'

'No chance,' the driver said, putting the van in gear. 'You might think this is Mad Model Movers PLC, but actually I have a regular day job.'

(It's my belief that, in the rarefied Hightechnicon world, sarcasm passes for humour.)

How to Write Really Badly

Joe's mother's cleaning lady raised her mop in warm salute as we drove off. The driver turned to me.

'Where next?'

'Walbottle Manor (Mixed).'

'I used to go to that school,' the driver said, running his gnarled fingers through his silvery hair. 'I had a really nice teacher called Miss Tate.'

'That figures,' I told him. 'Can we drive round the back?'

He knew the way. In fact, I'll swear I saw his rheumy eyes mist over as we passed the old school sign. He backed the van up to the fire doors beside the gym.

'I don't believe that you can open these from the outside,' I warned him.

'That's what you think,' he said, sliding a spectacle arm in a gap in the doors, and springing some catch. 'I used to break back in here regularly, after I left, to get to sing on Fridays.'

(This is what happens when you get a town without a bowling alley or a cinema. Everyone goes loopy.)

He helped me carry the models along the corridor, past the big hall, where everybody's eyes were goody-goody shut for prayers, into the classroom.

'It looks just the same!'

'I'm sure it does.'

And we set everything up. How Joe got all this lot in one small room, I'll never understand. They did fit in. But the huge water bottle mastodon loomed horribly over Miss Tate's desk, and Beth's angora rabbit, borrowed for the 'Textures' table, eyed the wall-sized tagliatelle spider's web with real dismay.

'Splendid,' said the van driver. 'A job well

done.' He patted his own particular favourite – the tin can baby elephant – with evident satisfaction. 'And this is sturdy stuff. I've moved top-of-the-range Hightechnicon Systems that will fall apart sooner than this.'

'Joe only uses the best glue and string.'

He glanced round wistfully, and sighed.

'I'd better go.'

'It isn't Friday,' I consoled him. 'So at least you won't be missing singing.'

He hesitated at the classroom door, looking back one last time.

'I spent the happiest days of my whole life inside this room.'

See what I mean? Spend one term with Miss Tate, and you go bats. Quite bats.

10
By POPULAr REQuest . . .

Miss Tate's bun shook as she clapped her hands. I watched for moths.

'Now, class!'

They sat smartly in their seats, like doggies waiting for bones.

'I hope everyone's got over the *surprise* of all these –' Nervously, she glanced up at the huge water bottle mastodon towering above her, gnashing his cardboard teeth. 'All these *wonderful* models that Joe has so kindly brought in to show us today.'

'I didn't br –'

I stepped on Joe's foot to shut him up.

'Because,' Miss Tate went on, 'it's time to award the prizes.'

She opened her desk drawer and brought out five rusty-looking medals she'd obviously bought cheap in bulk back in the Stone Age, when she started teaching. (As soon as I saw them, I realised that the van driver had had one exactly the same dangling from his rear-view mirror, but in the hoo-ha of the move, I'd taken it for a St Christopher.)

'We'll start from the bottom, as we always do.'

She unpinned the list from the wall.

'Best How-to book!'

Believe it or not, this went to the hard-boiled egg decorator in the front row.

'Best Reading!'

That should have gone to me. I *always* win best reading, whichever school I'm in. But I had blown it this time because I hated our Reading Together book (*Six Little Peppers and How They Grew*) so much that, each time she'd made me stand and read, I'd hung my head, and pawed the ground in my embarrassment, and mumbled so softly that she couldn't hear.

So I didn't get that one this year. Missed my big prize!

'Best Essay!'

Flora, of course. She came to fetch her

chipped old medal with a beam on her face, stared at it meaningfully as it lay rusting in the palm of her hand, and then started one of those ghastly telly speeches.

'The first person I'd like to thank today is my mo –'

Miss Tate cut her off pretty sharpish.

'I certainly hope no one helped you with the winning essay, Flora. That was supposed to be all your own work.'

How to Write Really Badly

Flora shut up then, and went back to her desk.

'Best Spelling!'

This one was a toss-up, I reckoned. I usually get spelling as well. But Ben was pretty good.

'Ben!' Miss Tate announced. 'Though Howard might have won, if he'd not had so much Hungarian goulash spattered over his book that I couldn't read some words.'

This is what comes of doing homework at home.

'And the last prize.'

Miss Tate was beaming at Beth now. Beth beamed back at her.

'Best Num –'

I coughed.

She tried again.

'Best Number –'

I coughed again, even louder. She glanced down at the list.

'Good heavens!' she said. 'I knew there was going to be an *extra* prize this year. But I never realised that there'd been a *change*.'

She read aloud from the list.

'Best Home-made Model!'

And all hell let loose.

'The spider's web!' shrieked Beth.

'No! No! The mastodon!'

'How can you *say* that?' Ben cried. 'That baby elephant is better than any of the others.'

How to Write Really Badly

'I'd swap everything I own for that lovely Wheel of Fortune,' Flora said wistfully.

'I've become rather fond of the octopus,' I admitted.

'Does that lampshade made of dried bread count?'

'The spaghetti tower!'

'It's not spagh –'

Miss Tate cut me off, frowning at everybody.

'I do think that, after all the work we did on Egypt last year, a few more of you might appreciate this beautiful papier-mâché scale model of the Valley of The Kings.'

My big mistake, of course, was writing 'Best Home-made Model' instead of 'Best Home-made Model Maker'. So the wrangling went on for hours, while Joe sat in a daze.

And, in the end, we took a vote. The disposable coffee cup spaceman won by miles. And Joe stepped up to take his medal with a grin as wide as the mastodon's.

'Congratulations, Joe!'

Miss Tate pressed the dingy old medal into his hand. He gazed at it as if it were some twinkling jewel. Then, closing his fingers round it and shutting his eyes from sheer rapture, he threw his arms around Miss Tate, and hugged her.

'Joe! You old silly-billy!' she said. But you could tell that she was thrilled to bits. 'I *knew*

you had hidden talents. And now I know what
they are, I'll be coming to you whenever I
need models to explain the maths.'

I nudged him as he sat down.

'See?' I crowed. 'Things are looking up
already. If you're busy making pyramids and
cones and tetrahedrons for her all the time,
she won't be able to spend so much time
torturing you into understanding them.'

His grin got even wider.

Now Miss Tate was patting the moths back into her bun.

'It must be time to welcome our Open Day visitors.'

Her hand was on the doorknob before Joe reminded her.

'But, Miss Tate! What about the extra prize?'

She turned back.

'Whoops! Nearly forgot!'

She took another medal from her drawer.

'And now!' she said. 'By popular request, and secret vote, the extra prize! For the Most Helpful Member of the Class!'

And she looked straight at me.

I went for Beth on this one, so I waited.

And waited.

And waited.

And finally, Miss Tate said:

'Well, aren't you going to come up and get it?'

'*Me?*'

'Who else am I looking at?'

Stupidly (considering that Joe and I sit in the back row), I glanced behind me.

'I mean you,' she said.

'*Me?*' I said again. 'Most helpful person in the class? *Me?*'

'I was a little surprised myself,' she admitted. 'But this was a free vote, and all the papers except one had your name on them.'

I looked around at them. They were all sitting, good as gold, looking at me with innocent, glowing faces. I felt a bit suspicious as I went up to the front. But the medal Miss Tate pressed in my hand didn't explode, or blow a raspberry at me, or shoot a jet of water in my face.

It was a real prize. No kidding. A real prize.

Don't think I'm not used to getting them, because I am. In his time, Chester Howard has won prizes all over the world for reading, writing, spelling and, once, for the most beautifully spoken Armenian nursery rhyme. (That was a fluke.) But I've never won a prize for any of those other things: Most Popular Member of the Class, Best Team-worker, Most Cheerful Pupil, or any of that 'Nice Personality' stuff.

I stared at the medal. 'Most Helpful Person in the Class'. Frankly, I've been in schools where the most helpful person could mean the one who didn't spit on your homework every day, or set fire to your tennis shoes, or beat you up. In Spike City Juniors, it would probably mean the one who threw your crutches *to* you, not *at* you, or helped you bury most bodies.

But here!

How to Write Really Badly

Here in Walbottle Manor (Mixed), it was like winning an Olympic Gold. These people weren't sinners. They were *good*. And *nice*. And *kind*. And pretty helpful *themselves*.

I couldn't help it. I knew that I was doing a bit of a Beth act, but the words popped out.

'I'm going to treasure this.'

Miss Tate gave me a little affectionate push, and I went back to my seat. As I threaded my way between the desks, I noticed that on every one there was a tiny home-made model, Joey-style. Robots and scarecrows and rockets – that sort of thing.

'Have you been buying me votes?' I asked suspiciously when I got back.

'Why should I buy you votes? I didn't know that you were making me that brilliant How-to-Survive-to-the-Very-End-of-School chart.'

I was pretty put out.

'How did you work out what it was? I was keeping it so secret I haven't even put it in the display.'

He tapped his nose. Then he reached in his desk, took out the security screen and set it up on the desk. Just as I thought he'd finished, he lifted a hidden flap set on his side, and then another, and then slid a panel round.

'Mirrors!'

'Sideways periscope action.'

'Cunning!'

'Worked a treat.'

(If I were broke, I'd sell this boy to Secret Services.)

I drew the How-to book out of my desk.

'So there's no point in hiding it any longer?'

'Not really, no.'

I handed it over.

'I hope it helps, Joe.'

He took it and stared at it the same way he'd stared at the medal in his hand. Opening it, he turned the pages, one by one. I had a sudden vision of all the squares I'd spent so much time counting and measuring and setting out, gradually being filled with bright brilliant colours that steadily and cheerfully spread across each page, from start to end.

On the back cover, I'd written in block capitals:

AND NOW FEEL FREE TO GET ON
WITH WHAT YOU'RE REALLY
GOOD AT ALL DAY!

(I'd been determined to get those magic 'You're really good at –' words into the book somewhere.)

He looked so happy.

'I don't even have to use felt pen to fill

it in,' he mused. 'I could glue a square and sprinkle it with glitter or dried leaves or –'

'I see it's going to be Mess-As-Usual around here.'

But he wasn't listening. He'd looked up to see the parents pouring in.

'Mum! Dad! Quick! Over here!'

They hadn't got halfway across the room before he was bragging. 'Mum! I won a prize! A *real* prize! Look, it's a medal!'

I thought his mother was going to burst with pride. And Mr Gardener took the medal from his son's hand and inspected it reverently.

'Your great-great-granny won one just the same!'

How long has Miss Tate been *teaching*? A thousand *years*?

Now Joe was thrusting the How-to book under his parents' noses.

'And look what Howard's given me, to keep me going!'

I crept away, before the Gardeners kissed me. I wasn't expecting my parents because, a whole lot earlier in the term, I'd noticed all the notes from school were clearly addressed to Mr and Mrs Chester (who are *they*?) and I'd felt justified in dropping them straight in the bin.

And I was halfway right. My dad did hear a rumour of the Open Day while he was in Harvey's delicatessen, but he couldn't leave his *milles feuilles* unattended any longer in the oven, so he couldn't make it. And Mum was slipped the wink by the van driver, who wanted an excuse to come back earlier. But when she told someone at the door her name was Mrs Howard, she was sent off to quite another room, and was delighted with the work she saw.

'Didn't you notice that I wasn't there?'

'Of course I noticed. It's just I thought that you were embarrassed because of that beautiful essay that you wrote.'

'What beautiful essay?'

'*My favourite book ever: Six Little Peppers and How They Grew.*'

I didn't get off scot-free, though. The van driver found his way back to our room, and he took a great interest in my work.

'Excellent, Chester,' he kept saying, as he leafed through my books. 'You've tried really hard here, I can tell. And this piece is good, too. Yes, I can see you've made considerable effort.'

He went up to Miss Tate then, to tell her all he'd been doing for the last hundred years, and that, even though I could clearly do with a little more practice with division, on the whole he thought I was doing really well.

'Oh, yes,' Miss Tate said. 'Though I admit his How-to book was quite a disappointment.'

'Yes, I agree. I do think he took a bit of a liberty with the spirit of the project.'

'Quite *naughty*, in fact.'

'Well, never mind. Most of the rest of his work is up to scratch.'

'Oh yes,' said Miss Tate. 'We're all very proud of Howard.'

The van driver looked a bit baffled.

How to Write Really Badly

'I was talking about Chester, here.'

'Chester?'

Miss Tate looked thoroughly confused. But, rather than worry the lady who had given him the happiest days of his life, the van driver moved away. I could have stayed to explain things, but Flora needed a spot of help carrying her new Wheel of Fortune out to the van. On the way down the steps, I asked about something that had been preying on my mind.

'Did Joe give you a model to vote for me?'

She looked me calmly in the eye over the Arrow of Opportunity.

'No.'

'He did give you a model, though, didn't he?'

'Yes.'

'And you did vote for me?'

'Yes.'

'Because he asked you?'

'No,' she said. And then, because she could tell that I didn't really believe her, 'But maybe because he did explain how very much you had helped him.'

I thought about it while she went off to ask the van driver if he'd mind dropping the Wheel of Fortune off at her house after we'd been back to Joe's, and then bringing everything she owned back to the Gardeners', in fair exchange. And I decided that, if Joe had gone to all that trouble to explain to everyone, then I must have been *really* helpful. I must have *deserved* the prize.

I ought to tell Miss Tate my real name again some time, I suppose, if we stay in this godforsaken dump very much longer.

Then again, maybe I won't. Howard is *nicer* than Chester, after all.

And, when you think about it, Howard's *happier*.